This book belongs to
a very special Nut:

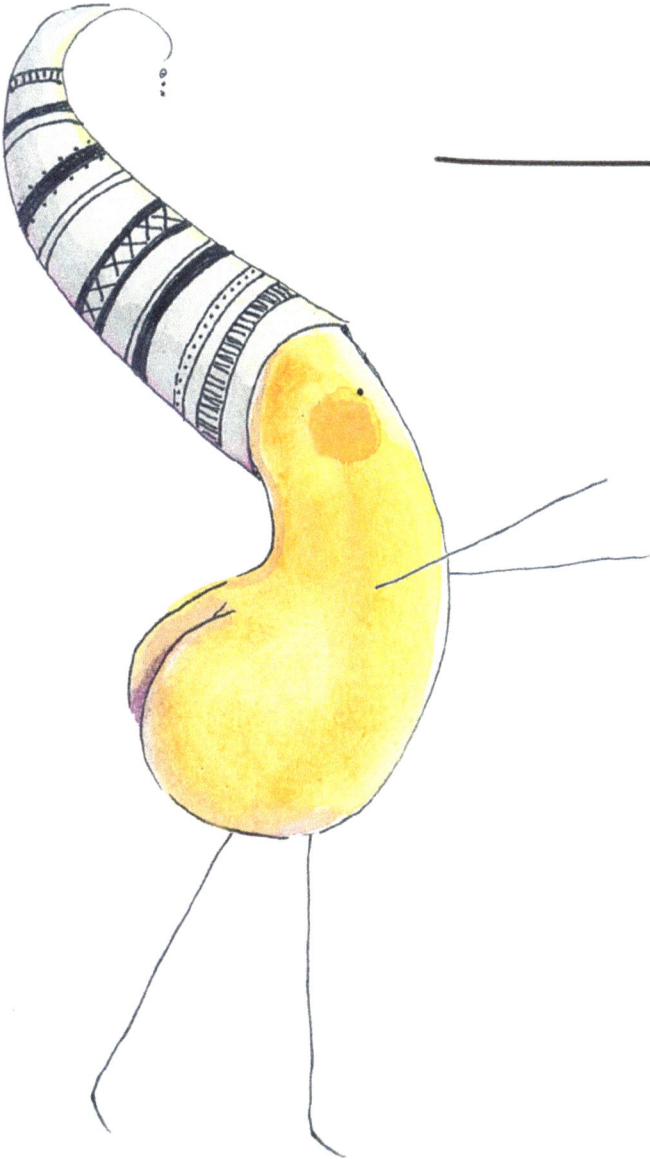

_____ ..

DEEZ NUTS

Written & Illustrated joyfully by Karen Feiling

We've got nuts that oversleep.

We've got nuts that see too deep.

We've got nuts that move about...

We've got nuts that can't help but SHOUT!

We've got nuts that can't commit,
and this little nut just CAN'T sit!

We've got nuts that
over-give

Being this nuts...

at times it's exhausting
and darn right
hard to live.

We've got nuts that ramble on..

We've got nuts that

TAKE IT ON!

We've got nuts that live with tension...

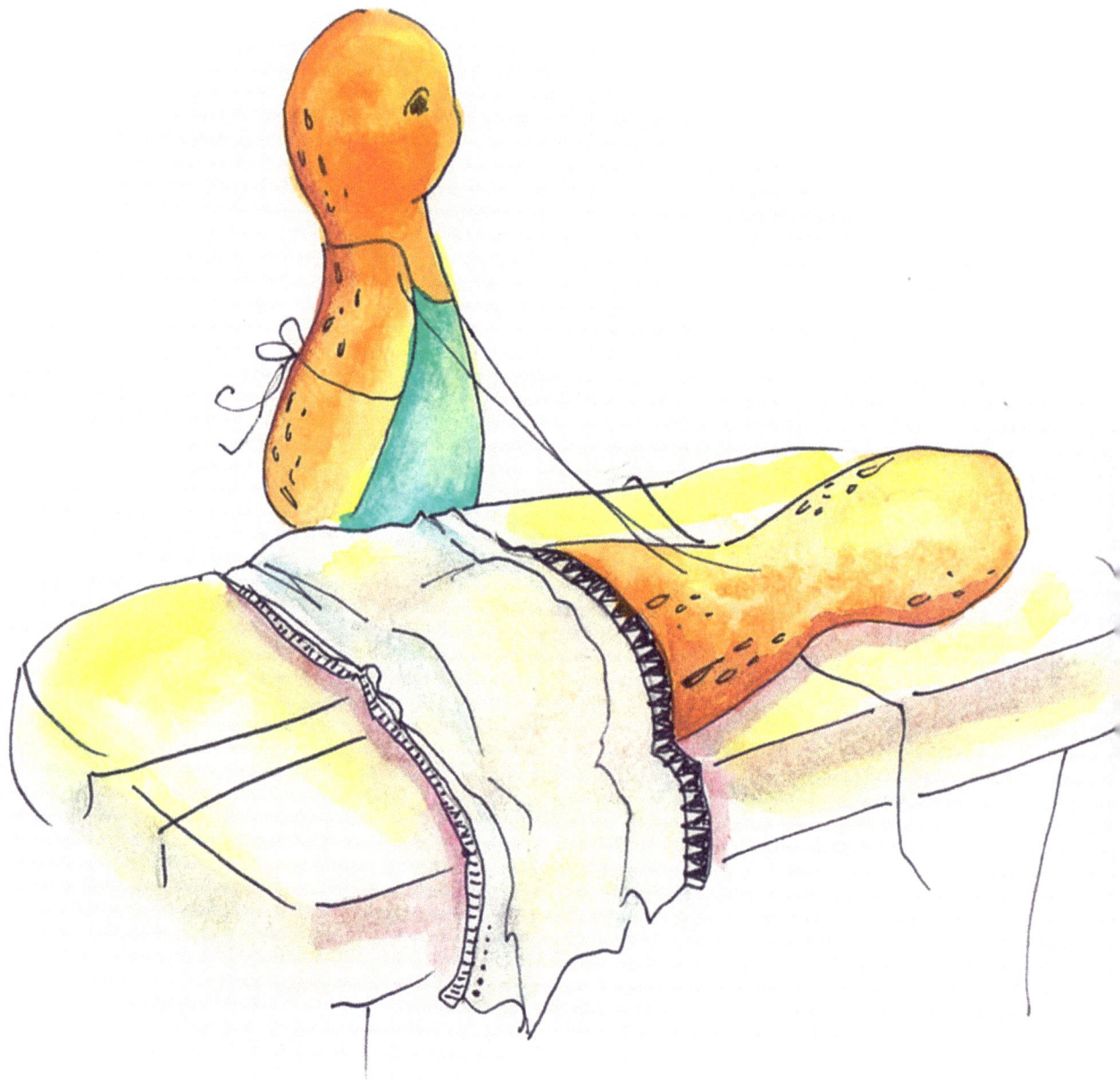

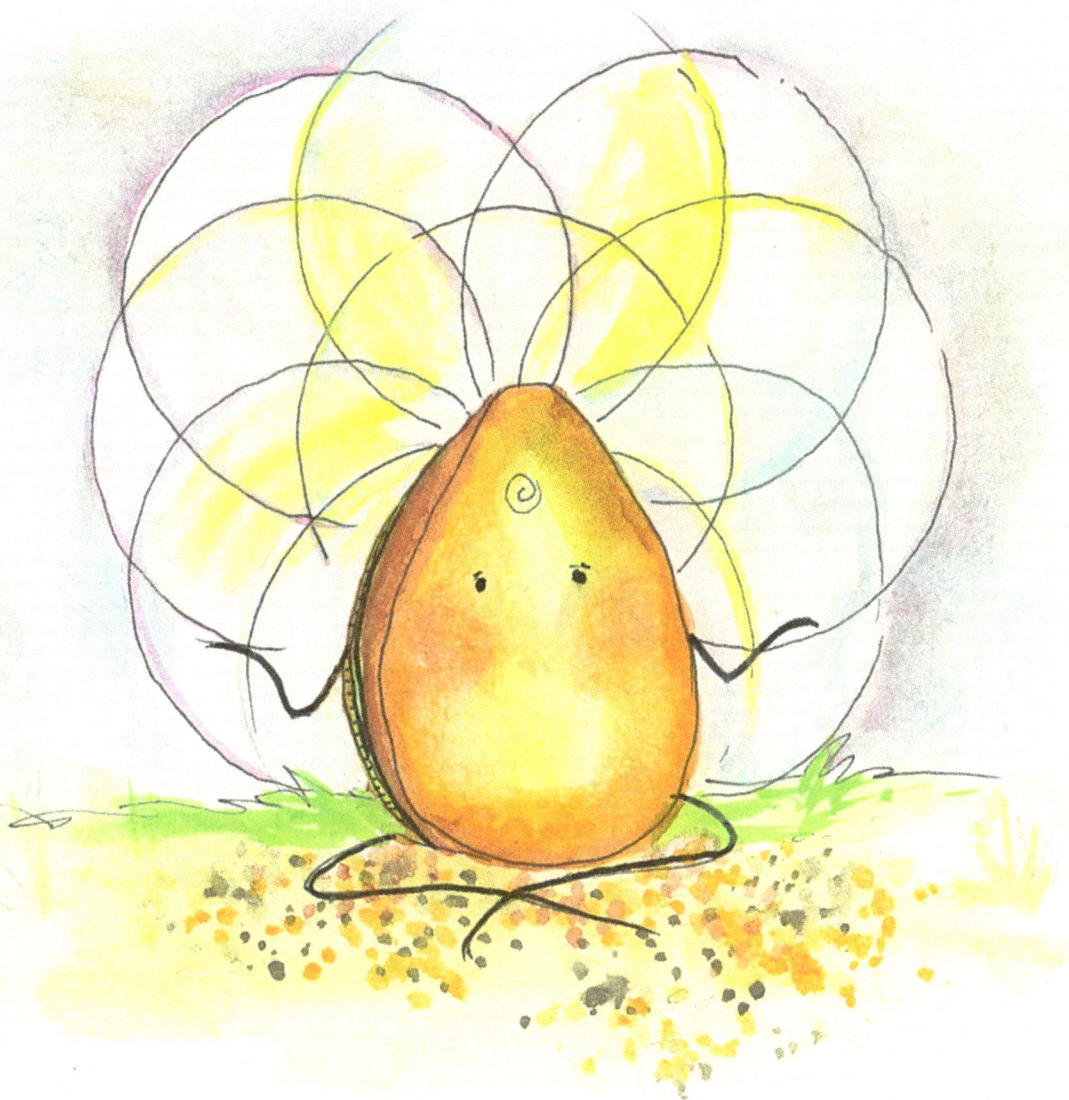

We've got nuts that have
GRAND vision!

We've got nuts with **EPIC** tales!

We've got nuts that bite their nails.

We've got nuts
that are easy to
EXCITE!

We've got nuts that stay up ALL night!

We've got nuts a little cracked.

The World's Finest Nutcracker
Self Doubt & Criticism

This poor nut is over packed.

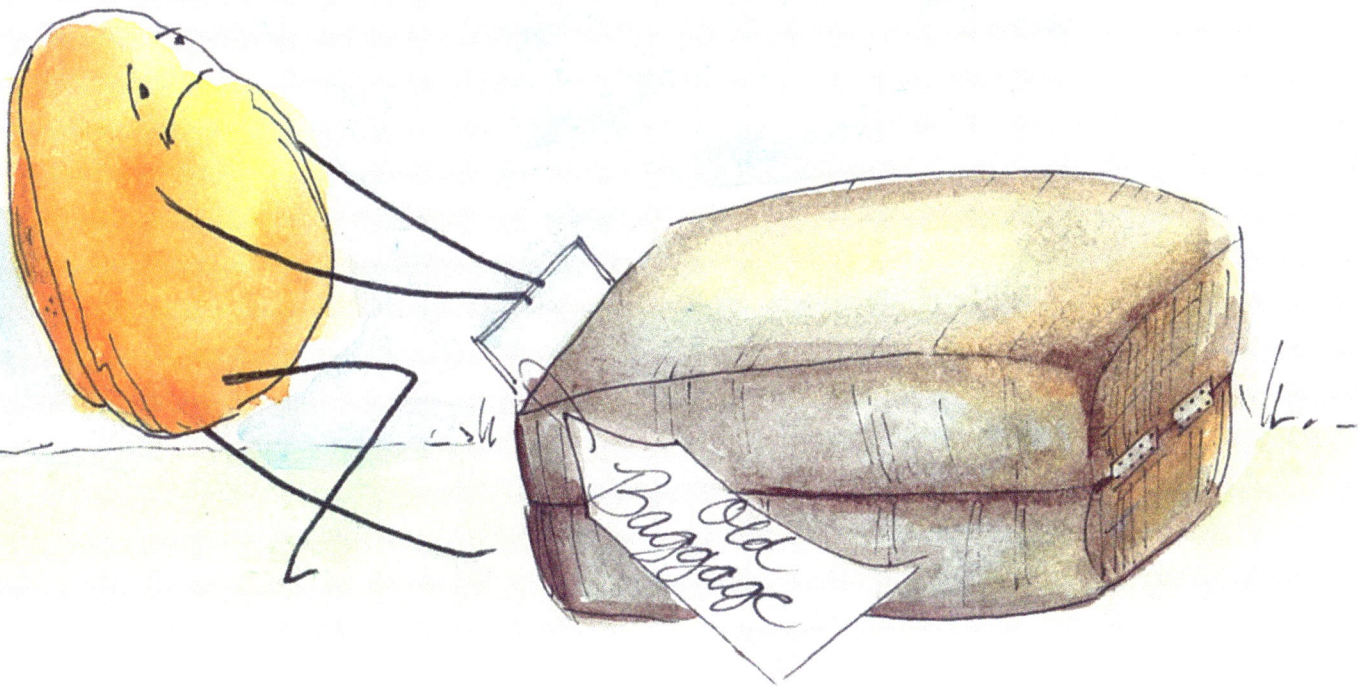

A nutty brain is **SERIOUS** business...

Nuts deserve
HELP, COMPASSION
and always
FORGIVENESS!!!

Nuts seek out their
wellbeing and balance...

And each of these nuts have
incredibly unique
TALENTS!

Deez Nuts is dedicated to all the lovely nuts of planet earth who could use a little genuine understanding.

Let your own exceptional
light burn bright.

You are here for a reason and truly the world is made better for it!

Be BRAVE little nut!

www.ingramcontent.com/pod-product-compliance
Lightning Source LLC
Chambersburg PA
CBHW040244100426
42811CB00011B/1145